MY SCHOOL

By Lauren Simpson
Illustrated by Ko San Tun

Library For All Ltd.

Library For All is an Australian not for profit organisation with a mission to make knowledge accessible to all via an innovative digital library solution. Visit us at libraryforall.org

My School

This edition published 2022

Published by Library For All Ltd
Email: info@libraryforall.org
URL: libraryforall.org

Library For All gratefully acknowledges the contributions of all who made previous editions of this book possible.

This book was made possible by the generous support of Save The Children.

Original illustrations by Ko San Tun

My School
Simpson, Lauren
ISBN: 978-1-922827-80-7
SKU02675

MY SCHOOL

Everyday I go
to school.

At school,
I have a desk.

My favourite
teacher is Mr Smith.

We learn maths
from Mr Smith.

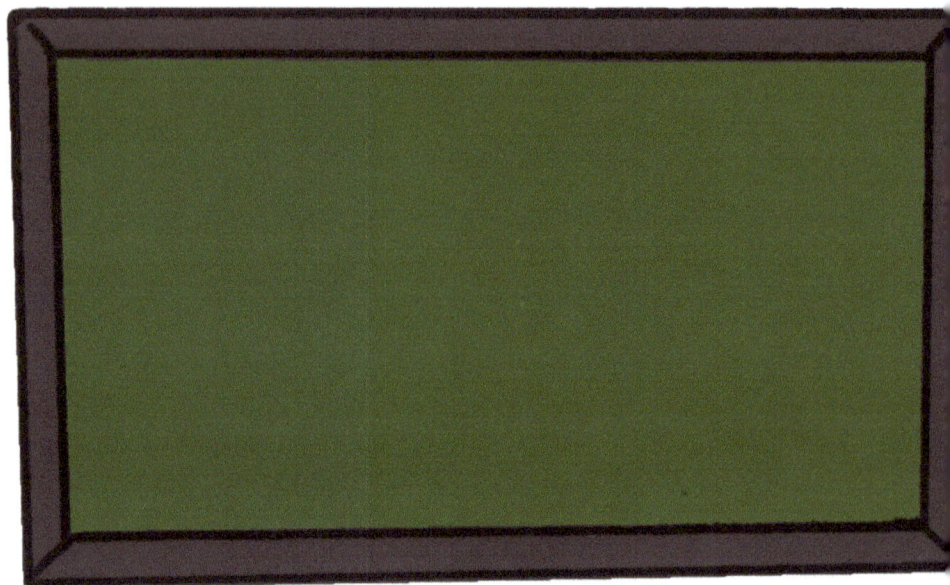

He uses the chalkboard to write.

Sometimes, Mr Smith
gives us homework.

For maths, we use
a ruler, pencil, and
calculator.

Plus, an eraser for
any mistakes.

I carry my books
in a backpack.

My favourite
class is art.

At the end of this year, we will have a graduation.

After graduation,
we will go to a
new school!

You can use these questions to talk about this book with your family, friends and teachers.

What did you learn from this book?

Describe this book in one word. Funny? Scary? Colourful? Interesting?

How did this book make you feel when you finished reading it?

What was your favourite part of this book?

download our reader app
getlibraryforall.org

About the contributors

Library For All works with authors and illustrators from around the world to develop diverse, relevant, high quality stories for young readers. Visit libraryforall.org for the latest news on writers' workshop events, submission guidelines and other creative opportunities.

Did you enjoy this book?

We have hundreds more expertly curated original stories to choose from.

We work in partnership with authors, educators, cultural advisors, governments and NGOs to bring the joy of reading to children everywhere.

Did you know?

We create global impact in these fields by embracing the United Nations Sustainable Development Goals.

libraryforall.org